DOWNSIDES

OF FISH CULTURE

The New Issues Press Poetry Series

Editor — Herbert Scott

Advisory Editors — Nancy Eimers, Mark Halliday
William Olsen, J. Allyn Rosser

Assistant to the Editor — Rebecca Beech

Assistant Editors — Allegra Blake, Jenny Burkholder, Becky Cooper,
Rita Howe Scheiss, Nancy Hall James,
Kathleen McGookey, Tony Spicer

Editorial Assistants — Melanie Finlay, Pamela McComas

Business Manager — Michele McLaughlin

Fiscal Officer — Marilyn Rowe

The publication of this book is suppported by a grant from the
Pharmacia & Upjohn Foundation, administered by the Arts Council
of Greater Kalamazoo.

The New Issues Press Poetry Series is sponsored by The College of Arts
and Sciences, Western Michigan University.

First Edition, 1997.

ISBN: 0-932826-54-7 (cloth)
ISBN: 0-932826-55-5 (paper)

Library of Congress Cataloging-in-Publication Data:
Lee, David Dodd, 1959–
Downsides of Fish Culture / David Dodd Lee
Library of Congress Catalog Card Number (97-67323)

Art Direction and Design: Tricia Hennessy
Production: Paul Sizer
                           The Design Center, Department of Art
                           College of Fine Arts
                           Western Michigan University
Printing: Bookcrafters, Chelsea, Michigan

DOWNSIDES
OF FISH CULTURE

DAVID DODD LEE

FOREWORD BY CHARLES D'AMBROSIO

New Issues Press

WESTERN MICHIGAN UNIVERSITY

This book is dedictated to Kelly Lee.

Contents

Foreword

David Lee's poems don't give us a picture of life lived per capita, life lived in the conglomerate heart or regressed to the mean, life polled and made plural—the old agreed upon world. No, instead, with these poems we are taken into the elusive, the simple, the hard, the resistant world, the one beyond all accommodation and comfort, the one we ultimately live and die in, singular as a pike with a Zippo in its belly. As an undertaking, this is spooky business, very intense and to my mind admirably quixotic in an age where wholesale numbness is available for the asking. And yet it is only in this singular world, approached brilliantly and without flinching in poem after poem, where at last enough clutter is cleared away and, with vision renewed and made raw, miracles once again pass before our eyes.

Some of the poems in this collection strike me as a mad search for the exact right word, the precise language, the image that will briefly put a stop to the need for searching altogether. Such a torqued up project carries an implicit threat of apocalypse, which is fine. For one thing it keeps the language harshly honest—you can't hurl pretty "poetic" phrases and hope these offerings will appease the beast. Take "Traveling"—a poem that's all full-blast like the Bhudda, as a man once said to me, a poem that carries us out beyond the "cardboard walls" of cliche and dead imagination, out beyond the still lit porch light and the pockets of standing water into a vision where traveling, speeding, the elusive green flicker of life itself, finds a last, perfect adjustment of insight, so that the hope of *arriving and having already arrived* achieves an exact balance—an exact hard-won, fragile balance, for adding another line, another word, even the merest sound, would undo the whole damn poem.

There are the poems ("First Turtle") in which a calm reigns frankly over the work as we negotiate the only legit deal language can make with life, clarity; and then there are the architectural beauties ("The Downsides of Fish Culture" or "Three Stories About Owls" or "1981"), ambitious poems that explore layers of perspective or develop a sideways narrative or test the reliability of memory. Again and again in this collection, David Lee tears the vanity mirror from the precious hand of language and forces poetry down a road more often traveled by fiction writers, turning the mirror around, as Fielding said, and holding it up to life itself.

And in David Lee's work, there is a consistent and thematic mood of aftermath. Is he giving voice to something generational? I believe so. How did we—those of us in our thirties—come to be on such casual nodding terms with death? In "The Auction" it is the young who arrive just in time to overlook

the end of things. The young in these poems are granted only a crude inno-
cence, a sort of trajectory. All that hard life, all the drugs, the screwing, the
crazy escapades—a proving ground proving nothing—unfolding in a world
come to rusting implements and the smell of constant death and the sagging
dugs of a dignified old woman. And this is why David Lee insists we see life in
the singular, and why these poems, vivid and vigilant, raw and urgent, speak to
our needs, because from now on, in this finished world, our miracles will come
to us out of the material others have abandoned. Nowhere in recent American
writing have I found such a marvelous evocation of a generation, the first to
be so at home with halfness and failure, to accept the end as the raw material
of life.

Charles D'Ambrosio

Acknowledgements:

Big Scream: "Traveling"

Black River Review: "The Mystery"

Cutbank: "Shot by Boy, Hawkins and Lee Die in a Flooded Quarry"

Green Mountains Review: "Which Comes Back, Delayed"

Lilliput Review: "Rope"

New York Quarterly: "First Turtle"

Puerto del Sol: "The Downsides of Fish Culture"

The Quarterly: "Sparta Rodeo"

Sycamore Review: "Chalcedony," "A Poem About Bluegills"

Sky: "The Auction"

two girls review: "Mount Garfield Road"

Windless Orchard: "A Poem About Pike," "New Life"

Yarrow: "Lake Harbor"

The author wishes to thank *PrePress Awards*, an anthology of emerging writers, for publishing a selection of his poems, chosen by William Olsen.

Downsides of Fish Culture

A Poem About Pike

Take the fork sitting next to your plate
and stab it into your hand. You're lucky you're not
swimming. The pike, like a shark, lives
for blood. A big pike will try to eat a full-grown duck.
They'd like to be alligators.
A pike's eyes glow in the dark.
If you catch one watching you you'd better pull anchor.
I once caught a pike in a ditch
and it had a warbler in its stomach,
and another pike, and a zippo lighter.
A man at work told me he caught a bass
in Pine Lake with its stomach torn out. A pike had gutted it for him.
The pike is a million years old. It's seen every craft
man's invented. It's too voracious for its own good
though, and will attack
a paint-chipped spoon dangled over the edge of a rowboat.
Its brain's about the size of a marble.
The best way to catch a pike is with a sucker
or shiner hooked through the spine.
In Indiana a northern pike mauled a child
playing patty-cake in the shallow water of an inland lake.
The clouds stayed pink for days.

Self Portrait

It seems appropriate somehow now
that I walk into the fields across the street
where the electric fences cordon
off the horses with blowing manes.
There's a paved thing, a kind of sidewalk
snaking into the hills alongside a fence
that eventually runs into a building
like a face with six huge doors
that must be for cars or huge tractors.
There you're stopped, clouds like love
tearing apart in the sky
that is the only thing left to walk into,
and I would, walk into that blown
nothing, but for this groundedness.

1981

1.
There's no sure way to get at that year, to claw it back into
    view
so it falls dusty through the damp plasterboard and unravels
on the cold linoleum floor from beginning to end,
but some brown water runs down the shaft of the hammer
and there's a smell like citrus in the air, one small piece
    of memory
running its hand through your hair.

2.
Splash this off the windows; the warm garden hose coiled in the
    long grass.
The year I painted one of my father's rental houses
I played an audio tape of the movie *The Shining* over and over
    again
while knocking wasps out of the cornice.
I washed the house with a nozzle. The sun shined for days.
Inside was the woman tenant's history, a stack of notebooks I
    discovered
in a mildewed closet, hardbound, everything dated.
I don't remember one thing I read in them and have tried
but am unable to keep a journal for myself.

3.
The snow today looks shattered and bone, streaked with long
    shadows.

4.
The snow today looks ground, like bone, blown into drifts.

5.
That winter snow fell for a month without stopping.
Muskegon mired itself down deep, butted up against the dunes
and I had been twenty forever.

Our coolers full of beer, we piled guns and chains into trucks,
plowed our way to the cliffs overlooking the White River
and shot whatever moved or just stood too still.
We'd sometimes split the dunes

of a midnight packed in above the moonlit ice
blinking shadows over Ergang Lake. We'd perch on the lens,
a humming circle
of snow-whipped light and radiator steam,
chop holes opposite the bulb beams
black as pinhole pupils, weeds like capillaries
waving in and out of view.
The impaled suckers writhed, like alternating parentheses,
before they disappeared into the black water.
I'd drink beer after beer
amidst the fog and light and flakes of snow
and imagine the pike suspended
in darkness just under our floorboards.

6.
The woman was pretty. She showed up one day
while I was painting her front door. I had a patch over one eye.
I got hit in the head
when the hook I'd strapped around a bumper
unclenched. The two trucks idled in the mud,
a hole in the middle of my windshield.
The woman offered me a Coke. Those pike. They flew out of the
    holes
thrashing. Later we boomeranged them clattering
into the bed of Hawkin's truck.
It's no longer winter but I'm painting this big white house
and there's only the weather—dry, sunny days for working—

and Lakeshore Tavern and the waves white-capping on
    Muskegon Lake
beyond the paper mill's vast parking lot.
A mile away men hauled sand out of pits in huge dump trucks
that thundered by
and shook the hell out of my ladder.

7.
You claw it out, it comes back different. The woman slammed
    the door
in my face. A paintbrush hardened
somewhere in a bucket. My car was full of beer cans.
For a year after that I painted the insides of apartments,
found pornographic pictures on top of kitchen cabinets,
grieving letters jammed behind baseboards. One time
there was a purse sagging in the middle of the living room,
    black vinyl,
looking stuffed with money, only when I picked it up
it was full of cockroaches.

8.
It snows all the time here.
The woman died—she was asphyxiated by a space heater.
I never met her
but I painted her house, the house she died in,
and I read some things she wrote.
I keep talking about snow because I went into the woods today
and for two hours
heard only the slish, slish of my skis
carving a path through the trees around Blue Lake.
There were men ice fishing, sitting on buckets,
and everything was white like that house I painted,
nobody at all living there.

Three Stories About Owls

The owls, two of them, handle all the branches in the
  chinkapin.
They edge through the tree
with their eyes open.
When I come near they fly off
and I dream of a naked girl smoking in bed.
I can hear in the snowy silence the sound of their gizzards
  grinding
the bones and hearts and light-struck eyes.

*

The corn stalks suck up rain, then stand freezing in the cold air
  and sun.
They become gnarled, like my elderly neighbors,
amidst stacks of rusty bed springs spattered with chicken
  shit,
their robes and slips tearing in the wind.

In winter their windows ping in the sub-zero nights,
a sound like the chains pulling the bones
of our dead livestock through the fields hung with lanterns.
A girl and a boy undress and kneel in cold milk.
The electric fence purrs. The old man makes love to his wife on a
  blanket of leaves
surrounded by pumpkins and Indian corn,
the T.V. crackling in the corner. When one of the local owls
  is struck by a car,
the woman, feeling a chill, moves over her husband, straddling
  him,
and opens the bedroom window,
which suddenly goes silent, warming up, ice crystals hissing alive
  through the screen
and onto her sexual body.

*

My lover has a ruler-sized scar
running like a creek
over her shoulder blade, through the valley
where her spine slopes toward her buttocks.
In the morning
it looks like a small mountain range,
red with white peaks.
I like to soothe her with aloe.
Whenever she brings a wounded owl
into our home
the deer out back stop trampling
the snow, their eyes reflecting
the color of branch water.
I remember hanging naked
from a cyclone fence, my wrists bound with twine.
Somewhere a radio played "Rock & Roll, Part Two,"
which is now a sports anthem.
The two track was lined with candles.
Anyway, the aspens argued beautifully
in the dusky breeze,
and a huge owl, infested with louse-fly larvae,
beat its large wings and growled.
The moon sailed through the sky like a schooner.
In this town we have the magic of tidal pools
and gravitational reversals
and the tamaracks exude what we call "tears,"
liquid the color of skim milk.
My lover exhales the smoke of her cigarette
over the cups of my privacy.
You're a beautiful child, she says.

First Turtle

(Wolf Lake State Fish Hatchery)

I'd never killed one before. I guess the best way
is to shoot them in the head with a twenty-two. But since
    one fears
what one does not necessarily know
how to do, I was in a hurry to get the slaughtering
over with. I sharpened a hatchet until it gleamed
then waited for the turtle to stick his head out again. The
    hit was clean but I missed
the neck and the hatchet sank into the turtle's skull.

When I was done I was blood splattered. The head lay dead
in the dirt but the body continued to move, not like a chicken
going crazy, but like a turtle with no head
simply trying to walk away. I picked him up by the tail
and stuck him upside down in a bucket to drain. When I re-
    turned much later
I found the bucket on its side and the turtle was gone.
He was fifty yards away on one of the dikes walking
    in circles.

One Week After the Oklahoma Bombings

Imagine the release of those few seconds,
the obliteration of all that longing,
the souls ascending through the falling dust.
Fuck the bomber, whose blood I'm sure ran screaming and hot
through his beautiful aorta.
He's lost in this fog like I am, not all that special,
still opening the shell of his eye
each morning to his own eventual death.
When the bombing was first reported
I pictured a map, a little mushroom cloud whirling
over the Oklahoma dust like a smoke ring.
In the meantime I watched a robber fly
intercept a leaf-cutting bee in mid-flight,
crushing its skull. Half an hour later
I'm walking through a government building,
the doors all closed and labeled.
Outside, in the middle of the city,
a man dressed in long shoes and clown make-up
presides over forty ripe watermelons.
So it's not such a stretch
when I arrive back home the tri-colored beeches I planted
are covered with Japanese beetles,
some of them riding piggyback, screwing.
There's a reckless and dialectical
progression unfolding around here,
the moths spitting paste on the hackberry leaves
the wasps eat and then die from.
Little cars fart down the road like toads
heading for a window well, a bed
of dead leaves and a tennis ball.
I know nothing about explosions, but once lightning
tossed me off of my feet and into a puddle,
my eyes so dry for a week
I used the cold metal of teaspoons to dull the pain.
Wednesday, April 26, the hot buds

have been burned yellow by frost.
The catbird's in its corner, crying, a hundred feet away,
and the monolithic Washington D.C. stirs,
its huge white buildings raining
little chiselfuls of salt on the shoulders
of the President and his assemblage of officers.

Which Comes Back, Delayed

1.
It's there now, in the light shining through the clouds,
not raucous, but pulsing with regeneration,
the rain drying up, the sexual flowers, the heat releasing
    new waves of pollen . . .

2.
Mostly I remember the unrealistic look and feel of it,
the young bodies burning with hormones,
the rolling water and stolen valiums and beer not yet
    clouding us over,
for we were venerable and in love with our
eternal collective youth, Hawkins actually pronouncing
what we all must have felt: "Our parents, what
bullshit, and they're nearly dead," and my appetite in those few
    seconds
grew enormous.

3.
And suddenly there was sun shining all over the boat, more
    sun than in Nature,
washing everything green.
And the blue-green fins of molded fiberglass and the rough
    stucco-sprayed floor,
and the orange life-perservers buoyed in a little water,
seemed dated and nasty in their pale glowing,

4.
something out of *Playboy*, the way I'd discovered it earlier,
stacked in my father's closet and concealed
behind shoe boxes and plastic suit covers,
the women all looking like Doris Day,
only nude on a leather couch. In the corner, a philodendron.

5.
How we laughed and laughed, girlfriends and boyfriends,
and coyly brushed against one another's bodies
flexing our arms and legs in our expectant immortality,

6.
and Hawkins: Hawkins and his back-flip
off the bow, the deadening thunk, and the hole closing through
    boiling water,
a swirl of weeds caught veined in a stream of sunlight.
The lake slid out from underneath us as all horizon.

I thought it was my terror
that brought him back, me squeezing my girlfriend's hand,
when he surfaced through the clouds.

7.
To say it was the day I lost my virginity is to ignore
the momentum of minutes
that carried us toward the insignificant coupling: the weird dolphin
    motifs,
the occasional deer fly I swished off her suntanned back,
and the relief we felt as Hawkins—bitching about the bump
on his head and popping a beer—confirmed we'd live forever.

8.
Shall I say we started with heavy petting once it came?
We outlived petting and necking.
I stuck my can of Bloody-Mary mix in a cubbyhole on deck,
and my girlfriend and I went down below, holding hands.

The Auction

The yellow field grass
is mashed to double mud ruts
running up the hill
above the vineyards that stretch from here
to Three Rivers. A man in red
suspenders conducts the bidding
from an old concession trailer
being pulled along by an International tractor.
Old men open black lunch pails,
women sacks of fresh peaches.
A bondoed-up Chevy sports a handmade wooden bumper
and a sticker on the trunk
that says "Don't Buy Jap Junk."
I don't really belong here
but nobody seems to notice me
despite my imitation moccasins
and lack of a cap
bearing a farm machinery company's logo.
An old man walking with a limp
stops to cough out a rope of yellow phlegm.
A big brown dog decides
to check me out. He sniffs my crotch
and moves on. I look at my clean
pink hands. I've only begun to live my life
and already I smell constant death
clouding the manure-fetid air.
A large woman with breasts
big as beehives beneath a floral-print sack dress
snaps for her husband to slow up
and he reaches back to help her over
a few dead twigs. She wouldn't
care squat, but I wish I could tell her
I admire the way she
lives into her old age, still picks her way
through rock-strewn fields

to look at rusty machinery on a Sunday afternoon.
And the old folks keep coming,
wave after wave up the trampled hill,
one step at a time, walking slowly.

Traveling

Sometimes I feel all out of proportion
to the tangible world,
my half-lived streets merely smoldering
among cardboard walls and pop-up trees,
but this particular morning strays
without leaving my basement,
up the window's mote-flecked stream and out,
where without a car I drive past a friend's familiar
brick house
with its lone motorcycle and still lit
front porch light,
and the celery flats, the flooded fields
on either side of River Road
with the flat-red ramshackle pole barns
sided with dented tin
and the automobile graveyards, the cars up on blocks,
doorless and empty (in the pivotal light
they look as if they're weeping),
through the rock-and-pitted landscape
that could be Gary, Indiana,
and up the downhill slope,
the fields of milk- and knapweed,
pockets of standing water,
brown grass, cattails.
Then Kings Highway, the still well-water pumped
village of Comstock,
and the black-haired old woman rocking
in a sundress meant for somebody younger.
More flat, blanched fields,
sumac, an occasional dogwood,
abandoned apple orchards
(the apples I remember were gnarled
and had worms—we'd climb the apple trees
and breathe in apple-scent instead),
while far ahead in the just-beginning-to-rise

heat, a period
turns into three flapping crows
turns into a dead raccoon,
eyes open and belly-up,
having died where the world funnels into
a miles-long archway of blowing trees;
oaks and maples and basswoods reach out over the road
as you enter the light-flecked tunnel,
and the open fields
snap in long horizontal distances
back toward the horizon,
because now you're really moving,
traveling,
speeding through the green, flickering light,
arriving, and having already arrived.

New Life

It wasn't death, but the afterlife I saw
when the branch skittered over the pavement like a tarantula
before my car. Look, I'm terrified
about God, how he is male, fatherly, calm,
thoughts that lead to disbelief.

One minute I'm kissing my lover, who is human,
her legs full of blood,
the next minute the vines are strangling the trees
to death and the man at the rest stop
in Coopersville is mouthing out smoke he's been so badly burned.
Forget it, he's dead, but it's not death
that's disturbing, not anymore, death like some smashed-up
    automobile,
but the pain, the poor man's previous pain,
and what is it good for if we can't bring it with us?

Afterlife. Is there sex in heaven?
Is there a language for pain? If you could touch an
    extra-terrestrial's head
it might feel rough or like motor oil
or like nothing to name.
There might be nothing to touch. Imagine intergalactics
    copulating . . .
We think we can picture something like that.

This summer, west of here in South Haven,
a man who wears Carharts claims he's been contacted by aliens,
the old unimaginative joke,
a farmer, divorced. Once again
what lies beyond this world has been cast in the light
of our simple humanness—an evolutionary extension
of what might become
if we give any credence to Darwin. It's that sketch we may as well
label MARTIAN in the dictionary—

eyes almond colored and outsize, cranium
big as a basketball, a withered pink body . . .
"It glowed like a plate in the sky." Sure it did,
little antennae crackling with electricity, a consultation
over your cornfield in Michigan.
Christ recently was seen to be weeping
on the side of a redwood stump in Mount Clarion, California,
little dabs of pitch
finally hardening into real pine tree tears
while the rock star head faded to plain old wood again.

Several bad days ago
I found myself speeding into the eye of a thunderstorm,
a bolt of lightning
igniting the trees, so that I got the impression
I was driving through a series of wreaths
twisted with grapevines strangling stunted poplars and aspens,
my headlights beaming through the watery planes
I kept approaching, never reaching,
and I thought of that man I watched die, burned up, his skin
    black and papery,
and now it seemed I was being visited by him,
dark in the back seat, who must surely be blessed
for his pain an eternity of peace, whose charred hand sought only
    his wife's hair . . .

A branch was tossed through the flashing
trees spotlit
between each stroke-shaped nimbus
flooding out of the marsh in high-beams.
I watched it walk across the street
of its own steady and slow volition.

The Downsides of Fish Culture

1. The Tank Room

You should have stayed in bed.
The Atlantic salmon sang this to me.
I turned the giant key
and the drain
widened its throat for the dead fish
and waste.
Then the sun came out
for the first time all winter
splashing vestiges of a month's
worth of moonlight
through the bare trees and all over
the snow on the ponds and dikes,
and the tide in the raceways
dropped off
breaking and shearing
the standpipes from their rivets.
What this did was catch me off-guard,
the reserve water supply suddenly
straining to fill up the system,
the balloons tight
against the floats
in the valves, so I had to crank
open the drain
and pull the screen
and the fish surged up against
the primary screen.
These aren't natural streams
after all and a single bolt of lightning
can send the fish
to the surface in an effusion of bubbles
and nitrogen gas,
and the most anyone can do is prevent the system
from tripping itself into a panic,

the screens in the monitoring
room flashing their green displays
for the code that stops the speakers
from howling a three mile wide bomb
scare from D Avenue West
to the walleye rearing ponds in Almena.
Whatever you do after that—
pull baffles, divert well water
for more fresh spring water—
the rust comes roiling
out the head like a deep brown oil spill
until the whole tank is nothing
but a muddy trough
reflecting anomalous strings of flourescent light bulbs
trembling and hissing their cold blue
veils of electric noise.
Five seconds without electricity
or, in this case, the momentary blazing
of the sun,
throws the water speeding
headlong with the force of gravity,
belching out rust and sphaerotilus
into nine and twelve ponds
until all you've got left is three feet of stranded
water looking back,
its surface suddenly pock-marked
with fish sucking air.
And they're stuck like that, the fish swim blind
between the slick baffles,
and the wind blasts hard against
the tank room windows.
At this point there's nothing else
you can do—the circling begins,
the eyes pop out
like lima beans,

the raw water begins to boil—
so you might as well put your hands
on your head,
because the fish want to die
and the ceiling groans
and every fifth brick bursts out of the wall
and the hoses all blow their seams.

2. Unloading Steelhead

It came like a wave over the hot
boiled earth,
the end of the first death,
the womb with the mechanized purr,
the truck almost like comfort
after the cracked walls
and scaps dragged
through black water,
these Godheads, these shadows
floating over the box
hurling the current so high
it was gone, only dead weight
rising and falling.
Well I was there
and it was nothing like the biologists say,
breathing in peaceful suspension—
the mouth splitting
then slamming shut
before the geological thunder
ran someone through the dark
speed into my side,

the water turning to shit
and blood
scabbing up on our gills,
a ticking like the crayfish
rubbing his claws
only louder, embedded in the earth—
because it was more like being dead
in a ditch
stacked full of ripening bodies
all gill-burned in rotenone . . .
I died a hundred deaths on my way to that final
death, the light
like a curved knife
moving through the dark river,
the dying fish
all flaring their gill plates
side-white on the floor
staring God in the eye,
or, eyeless, moving their jaws
to His private litany.
It was then I was plucked—
not Sturgeon Falls,
the painted weirs
nowhere in sight—
invisibly bound and hurled finless,
even my jaw clamped tight,
and my glazed eyes
dragged through something dry, hard weeds
cracking in smoke and gravel.
Then I lost my breath—
a too-narrow culvert
hugging me like my own purposeful
blue death—
and when I emerged
I swam where the pallets leaned

through clouds of fatheads,
the sand rippling
a poor imitation of home,
the water boatmen
scattering before me
like beads of dark blood.
I watched the dead
mouth the sun one final
hot breath,
the moon drifting overhead
like God's love
punching a hole in our stranded island.

3. Seining Box

In the end
we knew the blood
was God's blood
coming brown from the culvert
and snapping our scaps,
shredding the yellow wood
off the hoops for the webbing.
Then the boards in the stack cracked
and shattered
and the box filled with grinning
pike all ribboned in weeds
and laced through an ooze
so thick it could buoy
the crayfish who, lifting their claws,
looked about to fly.
The cement walls flowed over

with fingerling
bass wriggling to the ground
two foot deep piles
of reflexive breathing
and the sky turned black
behind the green trees
that trembled out thunder
you could feel through your waders
in the deepening mud.
It wasn't like we were working
with gene pools—
a weed grafted onto the spine
of a splake—but we were tossing
pumpkinseeds and mud minnows
into the grass to die
and now the one bull bass
we had placed in a washtub pond
drummed the tin
with his tail and breathed out bubbles
of black smoke
and the stack up above
cracked its cement against the dike
and the corrugated walkway
and bannister swung away
dropping bolts into puddles still raining
minnows and yearling bass.
We dropped our
smashed nets, hit
the aluminum screens we'd hammered
into the grooves,
then watched the heads
and tails emerge, some beating
the stacked clouds
some jackknifing up
and bobbing like clothespins

inside a huge hopper.
By nightfall we were dying
pinned to the wall
like it was a bed or a coffin
and I was so tired I only wanted supper
and a place to sleep
even though my partner was trying to talk,
his arms pulled way over his head
and yanked from their sockets, his eyes
wide open
until the herons came
and speared them out.

Maranatha

It was our friends who died
young raining through the trees
in the middle of the night.
Trimburger blew himself up with a homemade bomb
designed by Sullivan.
Sullivan said the pine needles
were talking and we listened.
A mile away Lake Michigan crashed
against the pier making sand
while the stars exploded
all around us
and someone said *There's Mark* who'd swallowed
a twenty-two barrel
and said in his note he was afraid
of the purple weeds.
We shivered in the leaves
trying to scrape out the sound of blood
pumping through our veins
when Boy came walking out of the beeches
half-naked and bleeding.
We all knew who he was, and we wetted our shirts
where the water shattered the moon.

Flood

How dry the death was
and when he spoke all the summer street lights
showed was coal
in piles and cracked into walkways.
Said he'd been to Alabama
and Tennessee, dug a cave in some foothills
there and lined it with paw paw leaves.
We sang stupid songs all night
just to forget the racks of men's ribs
hung over the river
most of us supposed were dug out of graves,
but you're careful anyway,
the bones wine-stained in the firelight
and clacking together in the slightest
hot breeze. Just up the hill was all the pavement
you could ask for,
working traffic signals, and an office building
dimly lit. We looked inside
and saw piranhas swimming
in a tank of green water,
bleached out and round
as country moons flashing through trees.
The telephone poles buzzed
overhead as we tipped a washtub of beer cans
against the mesh in the spring
that flowed cold out of Castor's Hill
and over the roots of the bear oaks
like out of the soft, lanced side
of Christ. We were just begging to be released
that night, the boy with death blowing
over his dry, cracked lips, the moon in his blonde
hair. We walked between buildings in black
coats then looked over rocks
a mile down into the blind gorge
and got out our small bags of white bread.

Notes From a Side Road

Just pray to God
When the snow comes down
The wind's not blowing

I've got so much love stuck in my heart
Blood is like that
It stops and just sits
In the center of the empty house

Mount Garfield Road

1.
Not here, where we walk like the living
trailing the scent
of the dead. I used to see what I am now in the headlights
    swinging
over snow-blurred fields of light . . .

shadows, trees,
the corn field broken to stubble,
and the long front yard.

2.
I go back, do I ever, to the day I was born. I steamed on the
    steel
table, freezing to death, my mouth and lungs burning, my skin
    bristling
with drying hair . . .

3.
She was on the fat side naked, but when her tongue used my
    name I knew
what it must feel like to ride a warm breeze
over a cold, ring-speckled pond in the evening.

He shrinks back
in the white poplars listening to the sound of Anna's leather
    jacket.
She stirs the pine needles.

He lights a cigarette and begins brushing the screens,
    nets and counts the dead fish
    nets and counts the dying live ones . . .

4.
That morning the minnows in the ponds went crazy and started
    swimming

in circles. The blue herons crying in the pine trees spread
   their giant wings
and touched them to their eyes.

5.
They took briars to the moon and thin lines thickened
with blood. He woke up naked and bleeding in the snow . . .

6.
We used to kill fireflies
by crushing their heads between our fingers
until the green light stayed on . . .

He unzips her jeans. She grips a couple of saplings and her
   breath steams out.
The sun breaks from between clouds
striking them both.

I remember the way the headlights shone
through the woods

7.
like the two blue herons I found yesterday trapped inside the
   raceway nets.
They kept walking and trying to talk until I knocked
their heads against the feeder hoods
and held them underwater. The fingerling trout swam up like
   bees
drinking pollen, their eyes shining through the bubbles, their tails
stiff with hunger.

8.
She touched my side there.
She lifted my shirt and sucked my nipple in the dark.
Her hair smelled like smoke.

9.
We held the males like machine guns
above the orange eggs swimming
in white buckets
and shot a little stream into each.

10.
Now: Sullivan produces a handful of sphagnum moss and rubs it
    gently between
the fat girl's breasts. She sighs. Some truck lights come on.
A car half-submerged in the pond spins its tires trying to
    back out.

11.
Anna filled a milk jug with beer
and we hid in the trees
finding deer runs to where the white sand glowed beneath the
    power lines.

12.
Similarly, I remember breaking out of Gateway. When I first
    arrived a man
who looked like Andre the Giant lumbered over
and hugged me
and my retreating face felt like a tightly wrapped bed.
The inmates groaned all night and an orderly went around dispensing
    large orange
Motrins out of a test tube.
When I slid through the glass the moonlight burned my finger-nails
and I felt like a ghost,
wild in the snow and headlights again.

A Poem About Bluegills

There are poems about bluegills. There are poems
about trout. The bluegill doesn't give a shit.
It'll eat a bare hook but would rather not hear
about your childhood. The bluegill's thick headed.
It hunkers down in the weeds, thinking. The trout's like a young girl
in a wedding gown. Touch it and it dies.
You can pull a bluegill out a pike's ass, it might
still swim away. I'm not talking about pumpkinseeds,
those little flecks of tinsel. The bluegill's
the stud of all panfish. People catch pumpkinseeds
thinking they're bluegills. A pumpkinseed shivers;
it thinks it's going to convince you it's cold.
Bluegills are fatalists. A slab in your hand may jerk its head
twice. Once hooked it goes for the mud. By the time
it's resting on a flotation device it's willing to die.
It doesn't grope like a rock bass, swallowing air,
the bluegill's a realist. It knows it's just a wedge of painted flesh,
heavy enough to pull you half out of the boat.
If you've got a big white bucket of panfish
sitting on top of the ice, the bluegill's the one still living,
thinking, its head like a stapler, mulling things over.

Sparta Rodeo

Half of the people wore lobster
bibs and drank out of paper cups.
I was in the dirt near a puddle listening
to the All Saw Razor Band
and smelling the hair on my arms for traces
of the girl
some fat black guy ushered away.
He kicked me out of her bed, which was just a mattress
inside a gutted trailer. Some of us
took acid and some of us drank and then
took acid. That night
a horse taking a shit was a marvelous event
and the loudspeakers in the grandstands
became the voice of God and we were the dead,
watching men heave wood boxes
for the girl who had returned and stood on a giant
platform with her breasts hanging out.
When she finally spoke into the microphone,
the darkness bloomed
like a freshly exposed, still beating heart,
and we brushed back our long hair
and stood in the mud in our shining clothes.

Nude with Northern Pike

1.
Some nights—tonight for instance—I'm all there is
while outside the sleet coats the trees,
layer over layer,
dripping down and freezing
until the thin branches run like fragile bones

through the millions of columns of ice.
The next day, of course, the sun comes out,
and the fire in the glistening trees

stretches for miles, arching over Wall Lake Road,
a narrowing glacial tunnel.
The beauty of all that! I can feel, even now,
the body's slow-motion drift
through all that's delicate and brilliant in this world.

2.
A friend had to tell me this morning the woman he's been dating
has brown nipples. They've been dating maybe
two months. He's been looking for someone to love

a long time. I met her when the two of them
picked their way out to where I was ice fishing
on Stewart Lake. I felt happiness for him then, for *them*,
for all three of us really,

standing dangerously on what was pretty thin ice,
dark ice because the water was dark,
8,000-ton cubes of black liquid, blocks

fused silently together beneath us, at least that's the way
I've always imagined a lake in winter,
a few fish suspended in each cube, the cracking and settling

of the shell of ice the only sound down there

until spring when the noises of summer begin to arrive,
the jet skis and outboards, the jitterbugs
wobbling over the warm skin of water,

the splashing of half-naked bodies, children playing,
women and men cooling off. "She has the most beautiful
brown nipples," he said, and wasn't smiling when he said it,
    dead serious.
I could have killed him I was so jealous.

The woman—her name was LeeAnna—was beautiful.
She knew a pike by its Latin name (*Esox lucius*).
I thought I was falling in love with her

that afternoon ice fishing,
just like I thought I was falling in love
over and over again that winter with three different women:
a local librarian, the girl at the bait shop, my ex-wife.

3.
When I was sixteen and ran away from home there was an
    abandoned house
I sometimes lived in that was like a cave, catfish skulls
nailed over the fireplace we filled with driftwood
soaked in gasoline. The walls were yellow,
piss-stained, and you could smell them in the dark.
An old gas-fed generator coughed
and sputtered in the only closet left
that had a door, so we could play scratched records—
Head East, Canned Heat, Robin Trower, R.E.O.

It was on the roof of that house
that I first saw a girl

completely naked and stretched in front of me
in the moonlight.

Sometimes she and I would stay naked all night,
smoke cigarettes and watch the dunes turn white
under the screeching stars and invisible gulls.
The record player boomed downstairs.
On a clear night we could look across Lake Michigan
to where the horizon bled shadows of vaporous
white dust, our own northern lights, where we knew Milwaukee was.

4.
On summer afternoons my mother's hair
came out of its hiding place. She wore red lipstick.
My mother cut my sandwiches across
not diagonally. She floated through the house like a feather
     duster.
For years I thought my mother had no body.

5.
One of the earliest photographs I have of my wife
has her dangling naked, moon-torn, the print pushed
to resemble night. She was the white of alewives,
her feet bent down and together
like Christ's. And I remember thinking, *You are the one*,
poised like a knife blade over the sand,
her breasts stretched flat across her ribs.
She was hanging from one of the wood structures
we built on the beach (we'd been reading about Smithson),
out of driftwood, bolted, what little cut lumber
we could find
at night in the weeds of construction sites,
some nearby houses no longer empty.
There, hauling boards. The light fell in double-slants

over her face and one shoulder.
She stopped once in that light. I remember behind her head
through a window
I watched someone's arm move in and out of sight,
window-light widening
across the plush black lawn.
We dragged the wood out of there.
That was the same night we pulled the truck
two feet into Black Lake just to see the minnows,
whole shifting clouds of them
in the cones of amber light.
Next morning we piled the rocks. We ran a dowel through the gills
of the snagged salmon. The driftwood blew,
its attached weeds drying to hair.
She took off all her clothes.
I remember rainwater had collected
in the metal tray for the ratchet pieces.
Her skin, flecked with sand, smelled like rain
that night. There's a photograph I took
that same week that has her buried to the thighs
in a walking dune, her legs nothing like
the trunks of the stripped oaks.
We piled wood into the bed.
The light would shift, each time, a V
over her. It turned into an echo.

6.
Halfway through a year old letter my wife suddenly breaks into
this cadence of photographic images:

Woman nude with northern pike

Nude in downpour, floodlit at midnight

Nudes strapped to trees, figures broken by foliage

Nude wrapped in torn inner-tubes

Woman eating dogwood petals

Flames; nude nearby half-obscured by smoke

Nude man underwater, seen through lily pads

Two nude women in high beams, thigh-deep in Black Lake,
frozen like deer

Woman's nipple and tree fog

Two minnows hovering, suspended under a scrotum

Two nudes in mist, carrying venison hindquarters on pole

Nude holding Promethea moth

Nude with bucket over his head, urinating, hands at sides

Nudes making love on a giant straw heart

7.
I suppose some of this goes back to the mother.
The hands cradling the head, the warm lap,
the reliable shock of milk on the tongue.

To clean a pike you slit from the base of the jaw
to the anus. The guts slip out in one motion.
Use a faucet and work the blood out of the backbone

with your thumb. I remember kissing Kelly

in the rain, wading reeds, fishing for pickerel.
The water ran down our faces

and some trickled into our mouths.
Be careful. A pike, sans viscera, can still swim away.
Chop off the head before washing in lake water.

8.
I still call my ex-wife once or twice a week
and sometimes we talk for hours. I visit my stepdaughter
(she's decided she wants to be a lawyer, go to Yale)
and we're all in the house together again.
Green tea, one of my paintings, the VCR still blinking
      in its cabinet.
We talk, my daughter laughs too hard at my jokes.
Upstairs, next to the bathroom, my wife's bedroom door
      remains closed.

9.
When my friend and LeeAnna left
they held hands walking away
(wearing mittens if you can believe that)
and I was left standing beside a bucket of minnows
and an ice strainer, one frozen pike curled like a giant
      horseshoe
half-buried in snow.
Writing this now feels sort of pathetic. *Winter wind blowing
my hair, the empty lake
like some vast salt flat going nowhere . . .*

But the rest of the day stayed beautiful, too. Frosted clouds
of breath, here and there a cedar blazing up out of snow,
the lake rimmed with small cottages,
one or two of which were still occupied,
curls of smoke drifting out of the chimneys . . .

LeeAnna. Inside one of those cabins,
while I spear another shiner through the spine
with a treble hook, a woman opens her blouse
and her husband or boyfriend goes to her.

Or maybe she's finished showering,
steam dripping down the bathroom mirror,
and she wraps them together in her warm, damp towel.
Maybe they just rock together. She musses his hair

while he kisses her neck. In the kitchen, coffee,
the aroma of it the aroma of dailiness.
There really is so much to look forward to.
Outside the sleet has turned to rain, it's pouring

in the middle of winter, the streets glazing over,
the branches bending and freezing and bending and freezing.
Tomorrow this will be news: "Hundreds
of Motorists Stranded: Southwest Michigan Iced In."

But tonight it's just an ice storm, and my neighbors,
alone or with families, get up from their chairs
and go to their windows, amazed,
thrilled by what's happening, bursting with love.

Rope

This good piece here
so much like a hand out of water
so much
like the father with one arm

Shot by Boy, Hawkins and Lee Die in a Flooded Quarry

We were dying and we were invalid,
the moths coming up off the water and all that blue dust
and the dusty beeches
swimming away from the holes
like falling rivers of noise flickering
under the shafts of the moon.
Boy was something else doing the dance
of the living right there on the embankment,
his belt of spoons singing.
His burned hands hissed in the rain
that stirred the leaves
poking inch-deep holes in the nearby Blueberry River,
or so Hawkins described it to me,
imagining it, drifting near dead on his back,
an old sassafras root in one hand,
the bird of his God in the other.
Meanwhile, I'd passed from flesh
but was still alive underwater.
I remembered my first walk near the quarry
as a dream I had in which my parents rode away
on white horses. Then here, with Boy dancing,
I could see the fleck in his eye that was like a window
and his nerves were on fire. Of the ways to be born
this was called drowning in sin, the slick uterine
roots twisting tight, the sunlight bleeding away
so that all I could hear was Boy
pretending to cry, his voice like a knife
cutting leather, and I felt the sight leave my eyes
and I moved my arms in the warm shirt.

The Thornapple River

I've hurt everyone now
and it reminds me of how Boy used to line the dead men
along the Thornapple River and cut their hair.
Most of the corpses were rotted
beyond recognition but their hair still grew
and it was long and thin and soft to the touch.
Meanwhile the river flashed and sparkled
over icy gravel, full of steelhead,
huge fish with pink heads who would stare you down
before vanishing into dark bottomless holes.
It was part of the fall ritual
to attach the hair to the spinners
and then just push the bodies into the cold river
and watch them sink.
The steelhead would go crazy, eating the flesh,
ripping the soft, delicate faces.
We'd catch them later with the hair of the dead
and they would gasp in the ferns
and we'd cut their heads off
and slice the meat away from the backbone.
When I left my wife I tried to do it with the same delicacy
I used to roll the dead peacefully into the river,
their eyes usually open but gelatinous
and indistinct. I'd fold the arms into their jackets
and re-tie their shoes.
But Boy used a pitchfork and he kicked the bodies,
sometimes kicking the head so hard the soft brains
drooled out all over the green moss.
I know the dead don't care, really,
what happens to them, being dead, but I can still
hear the sound of the winch dragging
them out of their graves
and I remember how they dangled from cords
looped into big beech trees,
spinning in the dark around the fire

like giant toys. I remember one man's tie,
how it floated in the breeze like a wind sock,
and how he made me sad, that man, still clean
in his nice suit, the sleeves on him flapping
in the wind like he only wanted us to cut him down
so he could walk back home and get into bed
next to his wife where he belonged.

Chalcedony

The dunes inverted the V the geese made
flying west. I'd get up, shake the sand out of my boots.
Whole afternoons passed as arrangements
of sand and sky. At night I might swim naked in the lake,
sometimes with a Baptist girl
I'd lure from one of the camp houses, away from her parents.
I remember once braiding a blind girl's hair, holding
the cherry-flavored joint to her lips in the shadow of a leaning box elder.
It was erotic as hell.
She held in the smoke. "Fuck my father," she said, blowing it out.
That day, from on top of the dunes,
I could see salmon chasing clouds of alewives
over the sandbars in Lake Michigan, swirls
like hurricanes drifting over a map of the world.
For a minute I wished I lived there, miles
from everyone but her, who was blind but had beautiful eyes.
They were like agate, cerulean-striped,
and when she pointed them at you it was like diving
into a river surrounded by high cliffs.

Watching Some of Them Live

1.
"It's all these twisty forms, like knots of pain. They remind
    me of the burn ward,
this kid named Keith in particular. He had holes for features
and the rest of him looked like melted taffy . . ." and she
    paused,
unhappy with the word "taffy," and you could see she was
    reaching
for something more appalling,
something that could at least approximate his pain
but she said nothing
and above the sound of the shushing water
I could hear her sigh. We were standing on ice made by waves
    in Lake Michigan,
the final ridge before a fifteen foot drop
into clear green freezing water
and on the outermost edge where the waves splashed up
rested glazed balls of ice
resembling human heads, oblong, and stuck on top of necks
melted by the last wet snow . . .

2.
My wife and I stood on either side of my sister where the
    three of us luffed into the wind,
a warm bangs-blowing breeze out of the southwest.

3.
I wanted to say I was sick of tragedy. I wanted to ask her
Why, if death's just part of the job description, is this case
    any different?
But I could see the deformities she saw
in the ice, the pock-marked translucent bands
twisting in on themselves . . .

4.
My sister says her heart patients die at the rate of about one
    every other day.
"Well isn't it difficult watching all those people die?"
She says it's worse watching some of them live,
the tremendous pain of just pulling in air,
the way the family crowds around the bed every day
with that look in their eyes that says, To die now would be
    completely inappropriate . . .

5.
She once described to me a woman
who had disembowelled herself merely by standing up.
She and another nurse had to pick up the entrails and stuff
    them
back into the body. "They were dragging on the floor,"
she said, "and strands of hair were stuck all over the place
and somehow a Dole banana sticker
I had to pull off—
She died, of course, about two days later . . ."

6.
She had nothing else to say about the hospital
so we just stood in the warm air
watching the sea gulls and listening to the ice crack and
    groan as it began to melt . . .
And then I felt something I hadn't felt in a while,
    I don't know,
but suddenly I saw the whole tableau—the arrangement
of us tempting fate on the edge of a melting cliff, the wind
    blowing our hair
all around—and it reminded me of an album cover (like The Who
    pissing
on that monument on the cover of Who's Next)

or the ending of a movie—the camera trucking sideways
    before pulling away across the water—
in which three people have survived whatever complications
they were made to face, and for a few brief moments they
    believe—
standing on now what must seem like the end of the earth—
    they could live through anything.

Lake Harbor

Once, from where I stood on the bridge,
I watched a five foot gar
swim by. It hovered above the green
motionless weeds, barely moving,
while the light around me shut down.
I don't remember if it finally swam out of sight
or if it just hung in the black water,
dead white, grinding its teeth.

But I do remember the air was filled with sea gulls,
hundreds of them calling and drifting
through warm updrafts. When the stars came
out I could still hear them and it seemed like the moon
I was hearing instead. I listened to the moon.
I watched it stand in the heat rays.

The Mystery

Hawkins and I used to catch bass in the Mona Lake channel,
huge bass torn from the pilings on light monofilament.

Across the river at Maranatha the Christians sang
weird songs about joy and ecstasy and everlasting life.

I loved the bass, their heads like big stumps
in the fog, their mouths moving in prayer.

Death On U.S. 131

I remember one summer
standing in deep grass near a big tree
and thinking *I am just so happy* . . .
Well, okay. But later
I became this *dark person*.
Just being alive counts for something,
I'm happy about that.
I ice fish occasionally and that gives me pleasure—
a big pike alive on the snow.
But the snow doesn't move me.
I stand back at car wrecks, secretly amazed.
On the highway once a dead woman
spoke to me. I almost thought
she must be comfortable
broken beyond decision
on the warm asphalt she claimed for herself.
The radiators hissed in the background like stage props.
I touched her right hand.
She died right while I was looking at her.
She was worried about her baby
who it turned out was fine, oblivious,
strapped snugly in his car seat,
but she was gone before anyone could tell
her that. In the meantime
the rest of us go on breathing.
Life and death, snap your fingers.
Sometimes I think, *There's a bluebird
on a branch*. I love the words.
But the bird—when you actually see one—
is the blue of the human eye,
flickering, going down.

After Lives

I used to be what the farmers around here
call a grub. Nothing but grubs, a fisherman might say
after failing to find any earthworms.
But now that I'm an adult (A large beetle
the field guides say. They also go on to say
I'm a poor flyer and that I don't eat.
Well, I choose not to fly because what I eat
is all over the ground, a bacteria
that develops on dead grass.) I look back
on those grub years with fondness.
Contrary to popular belief
it's the larval stage that's a blast.
After all, very few of us are lucky enough
to be born monarchs or tiger swallowtails.
This beetle stuff is simply the raw deal
that comes after death. Look. One day you wake up
so tired and numb even the bacteria
oozing out of the dirt seems pointless.
Before you know it you're deep in a shell
of your former self, you're your own coffin.
No more gorging on plant matter and sleeping.
Good-bye to all that! Sometimes
I'd twist in my cavern and stretch,
making each of my sections pop,
and then I'd doze for a week.
And there were so many worms passing by,
leaving deposits—I thrived down there.
The point I'm trying to make
is beware of your expectations.
An antlion came by one day
and told me to expect a great voyage.
Well I'll tell you one thing,
I'm sick and tired of walking all over
the place, and these big wings
are completely useless (that is,

I don't need them), and they're heavy.
I already mated. I popped out of the ground
and was face to face with a female
(who I must admit was alluring at first—
she had a long green stripe
running the length of her abdomen). Now I keep thinking,
What next? But mostly I'm just looking
for a place to sit down.
And I suppose that's okay—some peace and quiet
while I view the world from a stick.
But I'm also a little bit frightened
by my inability to make something—
a deep hole in the ground, a sticky bag of leaf bits—
anything to tide me over until the next life,
however ridiculous it may be.

North Carolina

There was the ground first, shaking. There were hands
and thorns, something in the vicinity of snow, half-bared skull
    of a deer,
a ditch with little water in it; white, hard leaves. Someone
    looped
a vine around my leg. Watching from across a field
    that rolled
and blurred with blowing snow,
I don't know where I went, unless I simply closed my eyes . . .

I saw a barbed wire fence steaming one August afternoon
I saw a barbed wire fence dripping fireflies
I saw a barbed wire fence tear a scarecrow in two

to open them thirty years later, the same snow outside,
North Carolina snow falling in Michigan, covering the woodpile,
the spruces.

    *

I remember the barbed wire fence dripping blood.
The birds down there had tongues, long thin tentacles that darted
    into any hole.
Grasshoppers big as tanks smashed
a swingset to pieces. A calico sheet wrapped
itself around a weeping man.
Spiders—some with wigs—flew against the living room windows.
And I—of a particular Christmas afternoon—was swarmed by gnats,
the foot of my bed
a harbor of cold entrails.

    *

Every winter the Muskegon River freezes over.
Once, fishing for pike, I discovered my boots

on either side of shifting altitudes,
and when I stepped back to the bank's side of what seemed to be
    coming apart

my foot punched through—
river water came bubbling up
and spread like blood surrounding a body,
a yellow stain
flecked with bits of weed still frighteningly green—
nothing ever changes under there—
and the ice groaned and split . . .

I fell for months, kept making it back,
clutched Lake Michigan icebergs
having leapt big stretches of open water;
chopped holes through one inch crusts still too felicitous
    to the shape of an inland lake,
the ice bulging under pressure
against the iron of a winter sky.

I shoved a ladder to a drowning man who never made it out,
his snowmobile still idling
long after the echoes of his final ripple
lapped the slushy snow . . .
I dreamed for weeks my own versions
of that man's nightmares as he sank, and there was no peace
involved, no oxygen-poor dissolving
into comfortableness and acceptance
thigh deep in freezing mud and weed sediment.

A winter or two later I broke
through thin ice anyway, and for a long time simply hovered
over a hole the exact shape of my boot

then
floating down
saw the head of a white sturgeon
impaled on a gaff hook,
a tangle of decoy wire
looping a nest around the slick of a submerged log
before I ever intimated any probability
as remote as my own death, an absence at worst
beyond the wonderful high of an adrenal flood.
Big fat snowflakes began piling up on the blue ice.
I clung for my life.

*

In Muskegon the snow covers the fields full of dead insects
and the cats run
unmolested over the newly packed snow drifts.
Lake Michigan sighs to the calm of another evening's lapped-up
    freezing.
The ribbed dunes dream beneath one another's shadows.
The stinking alewives are no longer a problem;
they've hardened, little spoons with eyes.

*

Barbed wire; wet, pulpy wood, leaves. I don't even know about
the snow anymore, or I never did. There were briars and voices.
There were boys

hiding in the woods in black coats. There was a dead crow
nailed through the eye to a fence post.
In North Carolina in 1964 the gas pumps in Rocky Mount
flashed their prices like flip cards
and I wandered through fields with a butter knife
wanting to murder cats, the cats screaming all night,
the cats like girls ripping screens.

Once I watched the Virgin Mary
rise out of my night-light, her hair dripping wet,
her mouth held out in her hand
and I ran till I cut my feet on the frozen lawns . . .

I don't know what I remember anymore. Where I was,
when I was young, I had a body hollow
as a sparrow's standing on a branch, whistling in the wind,
seeing everything, not knowing anything,
the crunch of fingers jammed into leaves,
the houses spiralling up toward the mountains
before rushing to line up along the shelf of the ocean, the
    heavy doors shut tight,
the windows sealed and flickering with television.
And that horizon just keeps bending—smiling almost—
cracking bricks, twisting fences.
In that far world the nighthawks are almost always bursting
    out of trees,
a little grass in their beaks, feet buried in feathers.
What I'm saying is I don't remember.
What I'm saying is the blizzard in Michigan had made its way to
    a warmer climate,
snow piled in heaps around a wide, muddy ditch
full of briars, my bare thighs whipped to blood
I decided I could live with in a world
so full of beauty and distance.

David Dodd Lee was born in Wellesly, Massachusetts and grew up in Muskegon, Michigan. He has worked as a park ranger, handmade papermaker and as a Fisheries Technician Assistant. He has been Poetry Editor at *Third Coast* and *Passages North*. He presently lives in Kalamazoo where he teaches creative writing and works at a hospital.

Charles D'Ambrosio is the author of *The Point*, a book of stories, published in 1995 by Little, Brown. His stories have appeared in *Story*, *The New Yorker*, and *Paris Review*, where he won that magazine's Aga Khan Prize in 1993, as well as in *The Best American Short Stories* and *Pushcart* anthologies. He lives in Seattle.